MW00682330

How Butterflies Came to Be

by Deborah November

illustrated by Gina Capaldi

Scene 1
The Old Man

Setting: Native American village

Old Man: Children, everybody is getting ready for the winter. The women are grinding corn. The men are fixing their houses to prepare for the long winter coming. Everybody is very busy.

Old Man: I am ashamed to say that the coming winter makes me sad.

Child 1: Yes, the flowers will lose their petals.

Child 2: All the beautiful colors will be gone. It will be cold.

Old Man: I have an idea, children. I am going to keep the colors of summer.

Child 3: That idea shows wisdom!

Child I: That way, the people can enjoy the colors of summer longer.

Scene 2
The Special Basket

Old Man: I will use my special basket. It can hold plenty of everything.

Child 2: We will dash around the village. We can find colors to collect.

Old Man: I will put this golden sunshine into my basket first.

Old Man: I don't want to boast, but everybody will be so happy when they see what we have done.

Child 3: Why don't you put a piece of the blue sky into your basket?

Scene 3
Collecting More Colors

Child I: Green pine needles would be good.

Old Man: Yes, and some white from the cornmeal that the women are grinding. I will put that in my basket.

Old Man: I love flowers so much. I will put flowers of different colors into my basket.

Child 2: Those purple, red, and yellow flowers are so bright and beautiful.

Child 3: The flowers are perfect colors to collect!

Old Man: The last thing I will put in my basket is the rich black of the earth.

Child 3: It is a great victory for you! You have saved the colors of summer.

Old Man: Everyone, please come here and see what we have done.

Child 2: Yes, come see the colors we have collected!

Child 1: You will not believe your eyes!

Scene 4
Butterflies Are Born

Child 3: Please hurry and lift the basket so everybody can see.

Village Person I: Beautiful butterflies are swooping out of the basket!

Village Person 2: They are every color of the rainbow.

Village Person 1: The butterflies are fluttering everywhere!

Child 1: One landed on my ear. That tickles!

Village Person 2: One landed right on my head! That feels so funny.

Child 2: The beautiful butterflies make me so happy, I want to holler!

Child 3: You must be so proud. We do not have to worry about the coming winter anymore.

Old Man: Thank you, child. I feel that I have brought joy to the village.

Child 1: Look at the colors! We have the golden sunshine and the bright blue sky.

Child 2: We have the green pine needles. We have the white of the cornmeal.

Child 3: Don't forget the purple, red, and yellow flowers, and the black from the earth.

Old Man: Can you see the similarities to the things we put in the basket?

Village Person I: The colors of the butterflies all came from nature.

Village Person 2: The butterflies are a gift of color for everybody to share.

Old Man: And that, my children, is how butterflies came to be.

Respond to Reading

Summarize

Use important details to summarize *How Butterflies Came to Be.*

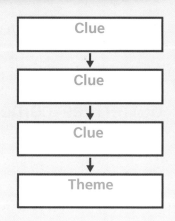

Clue
Clue
Clue
Theme

Text Evidence

1. How do you know *How Butterflies Came to Be* is a folktale? Genre

2. Why did the old man want to collect all of the colors? Theme

3. Use what you know about root words to figure out what *fluttering* means on page 12. Root Words

4. Write about what you would choose to put in the basket of colors. Write About Reading

Compare Texts
Read a folktale about a rainbow.

How the Rainbow Was Made

A man lived in a beautiful house with a large yard. One day, he looked at his flowers and noticed something. The flowers were all white! "I am tired of these flowers," he thought. He decided to paint the flowers different colors. He took out his paints and set to work.

17

The three birds living in the man's yard saw the pots of paint. They dipped their wings into the paint and flew up. They flew high into the sky. They did this over and over again.

The sun shone on the paint colors. The colors sparkled through rain that fell from the clouds. Red, orange, yellow, green, blue, and purple streaks of color appeared in the sky. And that is how the rainbow was made.

 **Make Connections**
How do stories help us understand nature?
Essential Question
How do folktales help you see how different cultures explain nature? Text to Text

Focus on
Literary Elements

Theme The theme is the life lesson or message in a story or play.

What to Look for Look at what the old man decided to do to make the people of his village happy. Notice how he used nature to create more nature.

Your Turn

Plan a folktale play about nature. What lesson will your play teach? What part of nature will you explain? Think about what your characters will do in the play. Write your ideas and share them with a partner.